2214 USWORTH SQUADRON

AIR TRAINING CORPS

An Illustrated History

DAVE WALMSLEY

And
The Cadets of 2214 (USWORTH) Squadron

FIREKAT
AIRline

Grob Tutor – Air Experience Flight Aircraft 1999

FOREWORD
OFFICER COMMANDING BRIAN ADGAR

The Air Training Corps came into existence in 1941 and, at the time of writing, 2214 (Usworth) Squadron has provided its services to the cadets of Tyne and Wear for over 70 years.

As with all organisations the corps has undergone considerable change over this period of time, both in terms of improved equipment and training as well as in conditions of service and working practices.

What has not changed however, is the ongoing commitment of the staff to the work that we do and their desire to provide the best possible service to the cadets we oversee. That commitment and belief was evident to me when I first walked through the door of a squadron as a tender recruit in 1963 and is still equally evident today.
The Corps has provided me with a lifetime of experience, family & friends for which I will be eternally grateful. Long may it continue.

This book captures, pictorially, this abiding spirit and I hope you will enjoy reading it and viewing the journey of 2214 USWORTH Squadron from 1941 to the present. I also trust that, for many, the book will bring back proud memories and will also be a source of information for those who did not join but who have an interest in work of the Air Training Corps.

Brian Adgar
Flight Lieutenant
OC 2214 (USWORTH) Squadron Air Training Corps

To all the Cadets and Staff of
2214 (USWORTH) Squadron
Past Present and Future

First published 2014

FireKat Ltd
Sunderland
Tyne & Wear

www.2214sqn.com
Copyright © Dave Walmsley, 2014

Published by FireKat Ltd.

British Library Cataloguing in Publication Data.
A catalogue record for this book is available from the British Library.

ISBN 978-0-9563871-1-0

Typesetting and origination by FireKat Ltd.   info@firekat.co.uk

Printed in Great Britain by CVN Print, South Shields, Tyne & Wear.

Contents

Introduction   6

Acknowledgements   8

One   In the Beginning   9

Two   1950's   21

Three   1960's   33

Four   1970's   73

Five   1980's   99

Six   1990's   107

Seven   2000   119

Introduction

The formation of the Air Training Corps really begins with one man's dream. That dream became a reality in 1938 with the creation of the *Air Defence Cadet Corps,* with the assistance of the Air League of the British Empire. The man was Adrian Chamier, Air Commodore, and it was through his foresight and enthusiasm that the Air Training Corps came into being on 5th February 1941. With it came the birth of 2214 (Usworth) Squadron, which has grown and developed into the unit we have today, over 70 years later. A testament to the man and organisations which had the forethought and fortitude to turn that dream into a reality.

Usworth squadron is intimately linked to the RAF station from which it took its name. Previously 'Castletown & District', it moved to RAF Usworth in the early fifties. Cadets had however been involved in its activities since 1938, and this continued throughout the war. Flights were available to cadets in a number of wartime aircraft. Use as 'ballast' in Avro Anson navigation training aircraft being quite regular. The air war came close to Usworth on 15th August 1940, during the Battle of Britain. 607 Squadron, County of Durham, beating off a Luftwaffe attack from Norway. Led by one Francis *Blackadder,* who later went on to command the Northumberland Wing of the ATC in 1948. Post war brought new changes and challenges. The change from being a recruiting agency for the RAF, the challenge to find a new role in a new world. This was achieved by modifying its objectives into those that would be useful in any walk of life.

Although numbers initially fell post war, the re-invention of its purpose, together with new initiatives, began to bring youth back into squadrons. This peaked in the late sixties/early seventies. So much so that an additional hut was required & built to house the large number of cadets on squadron.

The closure of RAF Usworth & opening of 'Sunderland Airport' was at the same time a re-birth of the flying aspects on squadron. The initiation of the 'Air Day' being instrumental as it brought in crowds from surrounding areas. This helped highlight the opportunities available on squadron and showcase the practical aspects of joining. Demonstrations by RAF aircraft such as the Red Arrows, jet fighters, transport & training types increasing the interest in all things to do with flight in general. Having the Sunderland Flying Club & Parachute Club on the squadron doorstep helped maintain numbers, despite its remote location.

The eighties saw the introduction of girls into the corps. This was not new to Usworth as it had a unit of the GVC - (Girls Venture Corps) on site, using the same huts on different nights. This later disbanded.

Squadron camps on RAF stations were basic fodder throughout the decades. The initial ones had the *whole* squadron departing for a week, to see the RAF at work & play. As well as viewing close up the types of aircraft on inventory. Changing from Hurricanes, to Meteors, Lightnings, Phantoms & Tornados to Typhoons. That is stating only fighters, the aircraft frequently in the backdrop of the camp photo tell their own tale of change, which is the RAF's story.

Cadets also saw their own air experience aircraft change over time, from Tiger Moths to Chipmunks, Bulldogs and finally Tutors.

Links to aircraft continue with the arrival of the Vampire gate guard in the 80's, Vulcan bomber wash in the 90's & the Phantom gate guard in the new millennium. Having NEAM (North East Aircraft Museum) on its doorstep maintains links to the history of flight in a more practical aspect.

Aircraft modelling - always a key part of cadet activities through the years, is recalled through the box art of *AIRFIX* kits. Many Ex cadets 'of a certain age' remember the action packed memorable scenes & exciting artwork that often resulted in a kit being bought. We thank Roy Cross for his inspired art & *AIRFIX* for the kits. It's good to know that both organisations have come through the decades of change. So that today's generation of cadets can carry on the legacy.

Similarly, the 'Air Cadet' magazine tells the story of the ATC from the early ADCC 'Gazette' to the modern digital editions of today. It celebrated 75yrs of publishing in 2013. Ex cadets helped in providing some insight into the squadron of times past with the documents to prove it. The new Millennium sees the squadron participating in the Washington Heritage Festival in its home town. Establishing a regular attendance in the form of a parade, band & PR stall. Whether it be flying, gliding, shooting, adventure training, DofE, sports, camps, or academics, the ATC has plenty to offer the youth of today. Usworth squadron helped to keep it to the forefront of youth organisations.

This squadron pictorial history has obviously been limited by the availability of photographs and restricted page count. A more detailed history of the Air Cadets overall is available in the book *'Horizons'* by Ray Kidd OBE (2014).

Our book shows snapshots, through the decades, of the history of 2214 (USWORTH) Squadron, Air Training Corps. In 2014 it is in its 73rd year of operation. From 1941 it has served the youth of the region with dedication and professionalism. Long may it continue to do so, as we look forward with interest to the next seventy-three years. *Venture Adventure.*

Acknowledgements

The following organisations and individuals are acknowledged for their contributions to this project. Their work assisted in the creation of this history. Cadets, Ex-cadets & staff of 2214 (Usworth) Squadron. Ministry of Defence, Royal Air Force, Air Training Corps, HQAC, Air Cadet Magazine, *AIRFIX/ Hornby* - with special thanks to Darrel Burge & Roy Cross. The Sunderland Echo, NELSAM & North East Aircraft Museum, Sunderland Library & Local Studies, Rolls-Royce, Coalfields Trust, Washington History Society.

Brian Adgar, John Allsopp, Joe Bosher, Derek Crozier, Robert Dixon, Fred Elliott, Scott Fiskell, Gary Foreman, Ernie Guy, Stan Hardwick, Dave Harris, Scott Harrison, Ray Hartley, Dave Ibbitson, John Kelly, John Killick, Graeme Leask, Larry Little, Dave Mason, Jamie Mcgregor, Stan Miller, Hugh Newell, Rob Norman, Keith Sproul, John Stelling, Sarah Stoner, Mel Turnbull, Denny Wilson, Jake Wilson, Jordan Wright.

We thank the professional and amateur photographers, for taking the excellent photographs in this book, with the foresight to see that one day they would be seen as *history*. Also the scribes, for detailing events & logging the changes through the years. Today we can present those records, pictorial & written, detailing those fleeting moments of Air Cadet history as it passed by.

Also to the Cadets & Staff of 2214 Usworth Squadron ATC, who *are* the organisation, for the work they do, to see that young Falcons may fly.

Congratulations to *AIRFIX* on 75yrs & to the ATC, that really started in *1938*.

ONE

In The Beginning

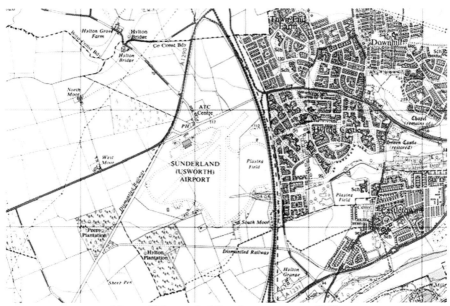

Map of Usworth / Castletown area c1960.
'ATC Centre' just to the North of the Airport.

ADCC Beret Badge 1938.   ATC Beret Badge 2014.

Above: **RAF Usworth Air Day 1934.** Air shot shows clearly division of base with accommodations on the North side of Washington Rd and grass airfield to south. Three Horse Shoes PH adjacent entrance with Westland Wapitis on display. ATC huts are today situated on the North side.

Opposite Top: The gated entrance to **Royal Air Force Usworth c1940's** from which 'Castletown & District' ATC squadron took its name on relocation. Previously thought to be located in a church hall at Castletown, a district of Sunderland. 'Hylton Aerodrome' had existed since 1916 and became Usworth in 1918. 36 Squadron (Home Defence) was stationed there with BE.2s and later Sopwith Pups. In 1930 607 Squadron (County of Durham) formed and Wapiti bombers, then later Demon and Gladiator fighters were used.

Below: **Hawker Demon.** 607 County of Durham Squadron RAuxAF. In 1936 the squadron was re-designated as a fighter unit.

Below: **Lamella Hanger.** Air Day 1934 (to L of photo P10) / Demons in storage.

Below: **Gloster Gladiator.** 607 squadron codes LW-D, arrived in 1938.

Bottom Left: **Air Commodore Adrian Chamier** is known as the 'Father of the ATC' as it was his original idea that led to its formation on 5th February 1941. He was also the main instigator, together with the Air League of the British Empire, in creating its forerunner the Air Defence Cadet Corps in 1938. He was thus familiar with the organisation and ideally placed to forge the amalgamation of the two corps.

Bottom Right: **'ADCC Gazette'** No.1 Vol.1. June 1939. The 'Gazette' was the first journal of the new Corps. This later became the 'ATC Gazette' in 1941 on amalgamation and ultimately the 'Air Cadet' of today.

Opposite Bottom Left: **607 (County of Durham) Squadron Crest.**

Opposite Bottom Centre: **ADCC Uniform.** Note forage cap/belt buckle.

Opposite Bottom Right: **ADCC Button./ADCC Logo/Belt Buckle.**

AIR DEFENCE
CADET ✕ CORPS
GAZETTE

The Official Journal of the Air Defence Cadet Corps

Published on the 1st of each month at Maxwell House, Arundel Street, Strand, W.C.2.

| No. 1 Vol. I | June 1939 | Price 3d. |

INTRODUCTION

Owing to the impossibility of finding room in *Air Review* for all the news of the Air Defence Cadet Corps, it has been decided to publish this monthly *Gazette*, in which will be printed all the news and information of general interest to the Corps. All officers and others concerned are expected to read the *Gazette* and make themselves acquainted with such information and instructions in it as concern them. Two copies will be sent free of charge to each squadron.

The *Gazette* will contain a monthly article on matters of general interest to the Corps, brief reports from squadrons, a list of amendments made during the month to Rules and Regulations, Routine Orders of more than ephemeral interest, a list of appointments and promotions, and names and addresses of squadrons.

Suggestions for the improvement of the *Gazette* are welcome, but readers are reminded that the *Gazette* is strictly utilitarian, and that the inclusion of pages of photographs and articles of general aeronautical interest cannot at present be undertaken.

CONTENTS

	PAGE			PAGE
INTRODUCTION	1	NEWS FROM SQUADRONS . .		7
GENERAL NOTICES . . .	2	ROUTINE ORDERS . . .		9
MATTERS OF INTEREST . .	3	APPOINTMENTS AND PROMOTIONS		15
FINANCE	5	NAMES AND ADDRESSES OF SQUADRONS		21

1

 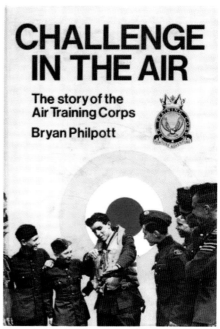

Above: **The ATC History Books.** 'The Story of the ATC' was published in 1946 by the Air League. 'Challenge in the Air' in 1971, both are out of print and tell the Corps history up to publication date. A new more detailed history is to be published in 2014 - 'Horizons' by Wg Cdr (Rtd) Ray Kidd OBE.

Above: **Model Making.** Flt Lt Jimmy Robson of the ADCC instructs. They will be used for aircraft recognition by wartime pilots. In 1946 he 'obtained' a Moth Minor aircraft at RAF Usworth which was used for air experience flying with cadets, until the CO of RAF Ouston commandeered it............

Below: **Inspection**. Mix of berets & forage caps, blanco'd belts & snow.

Above: **Moth Minor.** Advert for the 'acquired' Usworth Stn transport via J.R.
Above Right: AIRFIX **Founded 1939.** Destined to become a firm friend of ATC
cadets. Only made combs at the start, aircraft construction kits came later.

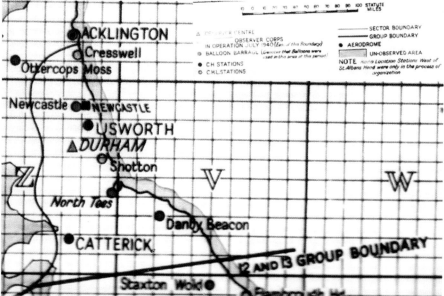

Above: **Sector Station. RAF Usworth** was designated sector fighter station for
13 Group in 1940. It controlled the reporting/deployment against air raids on
the area. CH/CHL - Chain Home⬤ (Low)⬤ are Radar Stations. (1940 map).

Above: **Blackadder Goes Forth.** Flt Lt Francis Blackadder was acting CO of 607 Sqn on the day the Battle of Britain came to the North East in force - 15th August 1940. He later went on to become CO of Northumberland Wing ATC in 1948. In the late 60's we shall see how this episode was played out in the 1969 film 'Battle of Britain. His aircraft can be seen today at RAF Hendon.

Not this one.   Air Day 1939.   The Few.   Memoir?   Theme Song.

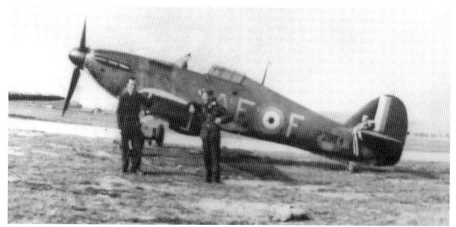

Above: **Blackadder's Hurricane.** No P2874 in 607 Sqn codes AF-F, taken after the Battle of Britain Luftwaffe attack on the North East, 15th August 1940. He shot down a Heinkel HE III off Seaham Harbour.

Above: **Hawker Hurricane.** Blackadder's mount. Full colour shows camouflage & markings to effect. This machine is on display in the Battle of Britain section of the RAF Museum at Hendon in London.

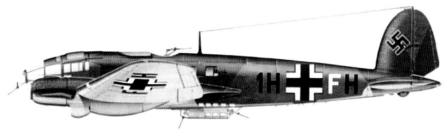

Above: **Heinkel HeIII.** of KG26 Luftwaffe attack force from Norway. 60 aircraft + 21 Me 110 escorts attempted to bomb RAF Usworth & surrounding district. They got a warm reception from 607 & 72 Sqns. Another 607 pilot, Harry Welford, celebrated his first 'kill' by flying down Newcastle's Northumberland street at rooftop height. See Robert Dixon's book *607 Squadron, A Shade of Blue.*

Above Left: **Joe Kayll.** 607 Sqn, was the escape CO at Stalag Luft PoW camp. Famous for its 'Wooden Horse' breakout that was later made into a major film.
Above Centre: **13 Group Crest.**   *Above Right:* **Rolls Royce Aero Engines.**
Below Left: **ATC Gazette** March 1941, Vol.1 No.1. The very first journal.
Below Right: **Alfred Ibbitson.** 1941. One of the first cadets to join the newly formed 'AIR TRAINING CORPS' on 5th February 1941. Later joined the RAF then came back to the ATC, eventually as CO of 2214 Squadron in the 1950's. He heard the original radio broadcast on the BBC calling for recruits.

Above: **ATC Crest.** Motto 'Venture Adventure' from ADCC logo.

Below: Air Cdre Chamier with Crest.   *Below:* Nov 1941 Gazette.(No.9)

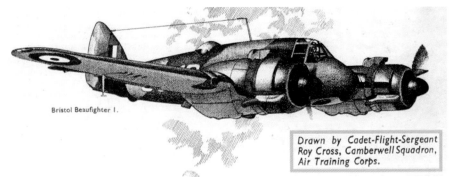

Bristol Beaufighter I.

Drawn by Cadet-Flight-Sergeant
Roy Cross, Camberwell Squadron,
Air Training Corps.

Above: **Beaufighter Illustration. Roy Cross** was an air cadet and had sketches published in the ATC Gazette in April 1942. He is more well known as the artist responsible for the *AIRFIX* kit box top lids of the 'Red Stripe' variety in the 1960's. RAF Usworth had a unit of Beaufighters stationed there for a time in 1943, (416 USAAF Squadron) these were night-fighter versions training with air intercept radars. The types 4X20mm cannons proving effective.

Above: **RAF Thornaby.** Annual camp, near Middlesbrough 1944. Aircraft to rear is a Vickers Warwick, a Wellington replacement.

Above: **ATC Button**   *Above:* **RAF Thornaby**   *Above:* **RAF Usworth**

20

TWO

1950'S

Above: **Kirby Cadet Glider.** No.31 Gliding School formed in 1944 at RAF Usworth and provided elementary flying training to the cadets in the region. This example at Yorkshire Air Museum, Elvington.

 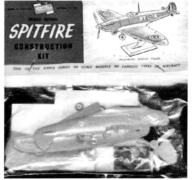

Above Left: '**Future**'. Sketch by cadet Benson Adams. Later went on to become Flt Lt in Royal Observer Corps, (*Macbeth*) then CI at 2214 squadron. (Page 99)
Above Right: **First *AIRFIX* Spitfire.** 'BT-K' a Mk1 made in 1953.

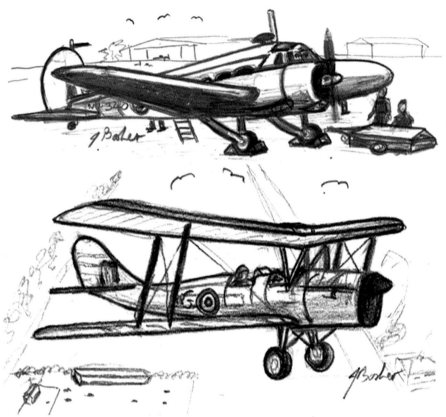

Above: **Avro Anson & Tiger Moth. Sketches by Cadet Joe Bosher** of his times at Usworth Squadron c1950. He went on to join the RAF, now he runs the 'Spirit of the 74th' website - RAF Halton Apprentices 74th entry Association.
Below Right: **Flt Lt Bob Storr.** The second known CO to take command of 2214. Period covered 1954 to 1956. At a camp at RAF Cardington in 1955.

Above: **Avro Anson WB461 at Usworth 1952 & Tiger Moth.** The 23 Reserve
Flying School operated Avro Ansons 'faithful annies' 1949-53 from Usworth.
Durham University Air Squadron, Tiger Moths. Both used for cadet flights.
Below: **Fred Elliott's 3822.** Training records to right - included 'Law & Admin'.

Opposite Far Left: **Squadron Stamp.** Shown as 'Castletown & District
Squadron' - RAF Station Usworth. Believed to have moved from a church hall
in Sunderland during the late 1940's. Original hut on Stn medical block site.
First recorded CO Flt Lt Cole in 1951. (no photograph)

23

Above: **F/Sgt Fred Elliott 3822 c1950's.** The Air Cadet Record of Service book. Flying log shows Anson, Oxford & Chipmunk aircraft with air experience, aerobatics & GCI (ground controlled intercepts) recorded. A flight in a Valetta WJ484 being one of the more rare trips, with 4.45hrs(!) to Kinloss the longest.

Above: **3822:** Fred's record book still shows the squadron as 'Castletown & District', part of No.64 Group (North Region) County Durham. Also shows 'A Ibbitson' as CO, of Flight Lieutenant rank dated 2 July 1953. Visits to RAF stations includes Ouston - air display, Acklington - RAF 'At Home' day, as well as camps, range practice & a 'flying visit' to Kinloss (Scotland).

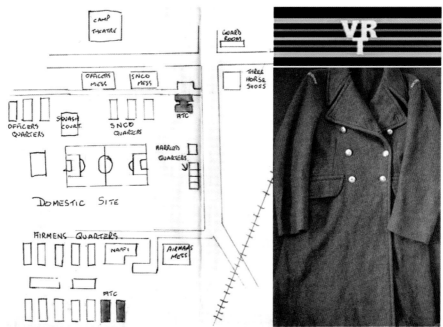

Above: **RAF Usworth North Complex.** Map sketch by Ex cadet Fred Elliott details layout of accommodations units. Blue details ATC sections, of which the building opposite the 3 Horse Shoes pub (Gliding School HQ) is roughly in the same position as the squadron HQ today. Originally believed to be the station sick quarters. Guard room shows location of the South side entrance (airfield) as shown on page 10. Married quarters is the site of today's Usworth Cottages. The complete South side now the home of Nissan car factory.

Above Left: **HRH Prince Phillip, Duke of Edinburgh.** Became Air Commodore-in-Chief of the ATC on the death of King George vi in 1953.
Above Right: **Duke of Edinburgh Award Scheme.** introduced in 1956.

Above: **Boeing B1 Washingtons.** More familiar as the B29 'Superfortress' in the USA, Britain acquired some on loan in 1950 based at RAF Marham. The significance is in the name *'Washington'*- Usworth is a district of Washington, County Durham, UK. (now Tyne & Wear) It is the ancestral home of George Washington, the first America president. The USA Washington is named after it, the aircraft got its RAF name after the place where the deal was signed. The RAF had a long tradition of naming aircraft after place names e.g. Lancaster.

Washington became a 'new town' in 1964 but the 'old hall' had stood on the site since 1180AD and was the home of the president's forebears. Original B29s ushered in the nuclear age by dropping the first atomic bombs.

Inset: AIRFIX B29 named 'Eddie Allen'. 'Enola Gay' dropped the atomic bomb.

Below: **Washington Old Hall.** *Below R:* **Washington Crest / Marham At Home.**

RAF Leconfield Annual Camp 1954. L-R **Front:** 6th AWO Anderson, 7th Flt Lt Storr (CO),13th Cdt Begg.**Middle:** 1st Sgt Young, 3rd Cpl Milner, 4th Cdt Moody, 10th **Cdt Hartley**, 12th F/Sgt Jenkins,**Back:** 4th Cdt Collier, 5th Cdt Rutter. Aircraft is a Gloster Meteor.

Above: **Wing Review Parade at RAF Middleton St George.** 1954 Sees the squadron on the march past (top) and at open order ready for Reviewing Officer's inspection (bottom). Berets have replaced forage caps but uniform is still old ADCC style.

Above: **ATC News 1954.** Developed by No.64 Northern Group, this eventually took over from the Gazette as the journal of the ATC./**50s Recruiting Leaflets.**

RAF Cardington Annual Camp 1955. L-R **Front**: 7th F/O Ibbitson, 8th Flt Lt Storr (CO),9th AWO Anderson.**Middle**: 1st Cdt Banks, 2nd Cdt Rowley, 6th Cdt Hall, 7th Cdt Elliott, 11th Cdt Rutter. In front of standard wooden hut accommodation. *Below*: **Percival Provosts** at **RAF Usworth 1950's**. A snowy scene with the Lamella hanger in the background.

FÉDÉRATION AÉRONAUTIQUE INTERNATIONALE

UNITED KINGDOM

WE, THE UNDERSIGNED, RECOGNISED BY THE FÉDÉRATION AÉRONAUTIQUE INTER-NATIONALE AS THE SPORTING AUTHORITY IN THE UNITED KINGDOM, CERTIFY THAT

Keith Sproul

BORN ON ...

AT *Washington Co. Durham*

HAVING FULFILLED ALL THE CONDITIONS STIPULATED BY THE FÉDÉRATION AÉRO-NAUTIQUE INTERNATIONALE HAS BEEN GRANTED A

GLIDING CERTIFICATE

NO. *23485*

THE ROYAL AERO CLUB

PRESIDENT

119 PICCADILLY
LONDON. W.1

GLIDING CERTIFICATES

Issued by the British Gliding Association under delegation from The Royal Aero Club.

THE HOLDER HAS QUALIFIED FOR THE FOLLOWING CERTIFICATES:

A. CERTIFICATE

DATE *21st October 1956*

SECRETARY
BRITISH GLIDING ASSOCIATION.

B. CERTIFICATE

DATE *21st October 1956*

SECRETARY
BRITISH GLIDING ASSOCIATION.

C. CERTIFICATE

DATE *23rd June 1957*

SECRETARY
BRITISH GLIDING ASSOCIATION

Above: **Gliding Certificate Keith Sproul.** Picture shows the A, B & C certificates necessary to complete the qualification. At the end of 1951 Jimmy Robson (see P14) handed over the CO's job of 31 Gliding school to Mark Scott. In 1955 this was renamed No.641 and in 1958 was relocated to RAF Ouston in Northumberland. 11 AEF and its Chipmunks soon followed.

Below Left: **Certificate Cover.** A young cadet Sproul in 1956/7.

Below Right: **Flt Lt Alfred Ibbitson.** Became CO of 2214 Squadron in 1956. Seen as a cadet on page 18 in 1941. Was in the RAF, then CI on squadron.

Above: **De Havilland Chipmunk - Air Experience Flights 1957.** A fleet of 50 aircraft were established nationwide in 13 flights. 11 AEF flew from Usworth. *Below:* **Kirby Cadet Mk3 Glider.** It arrived in 1950 as the first 2 seater. In picture below the Lamella hanger of Usworth can be seen in the distance.

1.Gloster Gladiator 2.Tiger Moth 3.Hawker Hurricane 4.Avro Anson 5.Bristol Beaufighter
6. DH Vampire T11 7.BAC Canberra 8.Hawker Hunter 9.Gloster Javelin 10.Avro Vulcan
(Now go out and Buy Them - and Get Modelling!)

AIRFIX Answers:

Below: **Aircraft Recognition.** How many can you identify?

THREE

1960'S

Above: **Red Hawker Hunter.** Camp photo possibly taken at RAF St Athan during a visit. Example believed to be the aircraft in which Sqn Ldr Neville Duke broke the world speed record at altitude on 7th Sept 1953. (727.63 MPH)

Above Left: **21st Anniversary.** Commemorative booklet celebrating the Corps.
Above Right: **Flt Lt Joe Taylor.** Became 2214 squadron CO in 1962. Flt Lt Alfred Ibbitson having to move from the district due to work commitments.

Above: **Battle of Britain Parade Sunderland.** Sept 1962 sees squadron march past town hall (top) with Flt Lt Ibbitson taking the salute. Bottom picture sees sqn at top of Vine Place, en-route to town hall in Fawcett Street.

Below Centre: **New *AIRFIX* Spitfire IX.** Released 1960, with new artwork, including fighter ace 'Johnny' Johnson codes JE-J. A 60's classic for modellers.

RAF Leuchars Annual Camp 1963

XH889

AIR TRAINING CORPS

INSTRUCTOR

Above: **Westland Whirlwind.** SAR - Search & Rescue helicopter. Leuchars camp 1963. CO Jim Taylor reaches for the rescue winch while corporal climbs into cockpit. Cadets are drinking bottles of pop (!) - the NAAFI van has just been around. If in colour the Whirlwind would have been bright yellow.

Below: **GVC with Officer.** Cadets with members of the Girls Venture Corps at camp. The GVC was a similar organisation to the ATC but for girls only. At the time the ATC only accepted boys - this later changed. The current CO Flt Lt Brian Adgar met and *married* one of their officers. (see p112). Aircraft to the rear is a Hunting Percival Pembroke (XF 797) communications aircraft. This was a replacement for the Avro Anson in service until 1953 (faithful Annie).

Above: **Tactical Exercise.** A parade before the initiative exercise begins. A young CWO Ken Horsley is to the front, dress is boiler suit fatigues with boots & berets. Possible accommodation buildings behind.

Above: **Initiative Exercise.** 'This is how it's done'. CWO Ken Horsley constructs a 'bridge,' while some cadets appear to be ready to do a spot of 'swimming'. Scene appears out in the wilds, Leuchars camp 1963.

Above: **Sunderland Airport.** RAF Usworth closed in 1958 to be bought by Sunderland Corporation for £27,000 in 1962. They re-laid the runways and refurbished the hanger. The 641 Gliding School, UAS & GCI aircraft had been moved to RAF Ouston in 1958. 2214 Sqn remained on site at the North side.

Above: **Dakota of Tyne Tees Airways.** There was an attempt to run a charter airline from the airport in the early 60's, which ran for a time. Possibly a shot of the first 'Open Day' of the new airport in 1964 for a small flying display.
Below: **Squadron Logbook, Committee Minute Book & Training Manual.**

RAF Kinloss Annual Camp 1964

Below: **Blackadder's Hurricane.** Outside the Ministry of Defence building, London 1963 - Battle of Britain Week. The same aircraft seen on Page 17 during the Battle of Britain at RAF Usworth. Not the last of its travels.

Above Left: **ATC Banner.** Presented by HRH Prince Phillip to mark the 21st anniversary of the formation of the Air Training Corps. 1941 - 1962.

Above Centre: **Convair NX-2.** Nuclear powered flight by 1965? The RAF 'Flying Review' seemed to think so. Mind you it *was* the *April edition* - 1961.

Above Right: **Air Cadet Magazine.** Now an A4 sized journal - shooting in 1964.

Below: **Avro Shackleton.** Aircraft on P39 at camp. A maritime reconnaissance aircraft with contra-rotating propellers. The Nimrod replaced it in 1969.

Above: **Wings Parade, Sunderland, 1964.** Cadets form a guard of honour colour party for the RAFA standard escort. Leading, NCO i/c CWO Horsley, cadets Hall, Hogarth, Wilson & Thorne carry .303 Lee Enfield rifles at the slope. White webbing belts complete the kit - with plenty of polish. Shot shows entrance to the then 'Bishop-Wearmouth' Church.

Above: **Avro Vulcan XL319.** Issued to 617 (the Dambusters) Squadron in 1961. This aircraft (nearest in photo) in 'anti-flash' white, would have been on alert as Britain's nuclear deterrent during the Cuban Missile Crisis of 1962. Part of the 'V' Bomber force it finally came to land at the then Sunderland (Usworth) Airport in 1983. It can still be seen as part of the Aircraft Museums exhibits.

Each year a number of selected ATC cadets go to the Far East in RAF Transport Command aircraft. They are crew members and travel as assistant quartermasters. 3 who recently went were, left to right, Cdt. W.O. K. Horsley, 2214 (Castletown) Sqn., Cdt. F.S. G. Wilson, 1138 (Ardrossan) Sqn., and Cdt. Cpl. B. Poole, 171 (Christchurch) Sqn. During 1964 a total of 70 cadets made the exciting trip which took them from Lyneham through the Near East, Gan and Singapore where they spent two or three days.

Above Left: **Air Cadet Magazine 1964.** Under the title of 'Overseas Flights'. Notice the squadron is still referred to as 'Castletown' although by this time had moved to Usworth. CWO Horsley goes on to become an officer at 2214.

Above Right: **Far East Air Force & RAF Gan Crests.** Both now history.

Above& Below: **RAF Ouston Shooting Detail 1965.** Available while at AEF.

Below Left: **.303 Lee Enfield.** Standard weapon for target shooting in the 60's.

THIS IS THE AIR TRAINING CORPS

'VENTURE ADVENTURE'

51 years of famous warplanes

43

Above: **TSR.2 XR219 1965.** Allegedly the best aircraft the RAF never had. The Tactical/Strike/Reconnaissance   aircraft was to be at the cutting edge of technology in 1965. It featured terrain following radar and advanced 'black boxes' with highly developed recon cameras. The government cancelled it.

Leslie Crickmore   *Above: AIRFIX* **TSR2.** Arrived in 2005 1:48 scale later.

Below: **(US) RAF F-111K.** The government's weapon of choice. The RAF was to be supplied with the American F-111'K' version of the new 'swing-wing' bomber when TSR2 was cancelled. Due to cost overruns & delays this too was cancelled. Leaving no replacement for the long serving Canberra.

Battle of Britain Souvenir Books 1963/4. Heralding the *'Most advanced Tactical Strike Reconnaissance Aircraft in the World.'* It was not to be.

Opposite Left: **Leslie Crickmore**. Was one of the team working on TSR2 developing camera lens designs. He was quoted as saying *" I had designed a lens that could capture the Snap, Crackle & Pop in your breakfast cereal".* He came from South Hylton (Sunderland) which is adjacent Castletown district. The technology/research later went into the Tornado strike aircraft & Concorde airliner. Les later researched and developed 'Animutation' - the moving weather picture we now see on our screens. He died aged 87 in 2010.

Below: **TSR.2 Model**. Showing how the aircraft might have looked in squadron service alongside the Tornado with camouflage replacing anti-flash white.

Above: **Wing Sports Day Blaydon Grammar School 1965.** Flt Lt Taylor of Usworth squadron (left with glasses) judging the long jump.

Above: **RAF Cranwell North Regional Sports 1965.** Cadet Dalzell in the one mile race final. Cadets progressed from Wing heats to national events.

Above: **Squadron Parade 1967.** Photo shows grassed compound area (facing east) at Usworth. Sports playing fields can be seen behind in the direction of Castletown, - to be the site of the Aircraft Museum. The parade is standing on the area that will become the site for the Vampire gate guardian, which will appear in the '80s. Hedge shows line of Washington Road running L to R.

13-17? You could be an Air Cadet

Above: **ATC Advert 1967** Advertising the many advantages of becoming an Air Cadet. Coupon would deliver leaflet with address of nearest squadron.

Above: **RAF Ouston AEF Chipmunk 1967.** 11 Air Experience Flight arrived at Ouston in 1958 and operated from there until they moved to RAF Leeming in 1974. Cadet is being strapped in rear seat of cockpit. To the left is a fuel bowser, to the right the hanger doors. The building to the rear is the 'Safety Equipment Section'. The cadet transport bus can just be seen to the right of this in the distance. Day-Glo stripes can be seen on the aircraft nose.

Above: **RAF Ouston AEF - Waiting to Fly 1967.** At this time it was not unusual to have 15+ cadets from the squadron to go flying. .303 shooting was often combined with this. The cadet 'greatcoat' was still worn outside the hanger.

Above: **RAF Ouston.**

Above: **DH Chipmunk.**

48

Above Left: **Kitted Out.** Parachute at the ready - awaiting orders to fly.
Above Right: **RAF Ouston Crest.** Roman helm a nod to adjacent Roman Wall.

Above: **Alternative Flight - Usworth.** Senior Cadet Lee prepares for a flight in a Victa aircraft belonging to Sunderland Flying Club. As the Sunderland Airport was only over the road from Sqn HQ these 'hops' were not infrequent.

Above: AIRFIX **Chipmunk.**   *Above:* **RAF Ouston.**

Above: **RAF Machrihanish.** *Back* from L- Cdts Cpl Colin Usher, David Hughes, Rob Norman, Cargill, Gordon, David Pinman, Ray Seaman, Valentine, Jim Clark. *Centre* from L- Sgt Colin Bailey, Sgt John English, CI Harry Hogarth, Flt Lt Jones, Plt Off Horsley, CWO Colin Lee, Sgt Reggie Bridge. *Front* from L- Cdt Abbass, (?) (?) Stephen Tye, Duffy, Cpl Brown, (?).

Above L: **Medal Men.** Wg Cmdr Gowing (Durham Wing CO), Group Captain & CO Flt Lt Jones prior to Sqn inspection. Note rows of medals, many officers were Ex forces and often had awards from the war years,3 Horse Shoes at rear
Above R: **Air Cadet 1966 (9d). / Flying Officers Rank Braid & gilt VRT badge.**
Opposite: **RAF Wyton Annual Camp 1968.** Victor 'V' Bomber at rear.

Above: **Air Day 67 at Sunderland Airport.** The airport 'open day' in 1964 continued as an annual event with a series of air days. A Red Arrow Folland Gnat bursts through the front cover of the program - which Cadets sold (!)

Above Left: **Control Tower at Usworth.** Mr B. Hurn in charge of traffic control.
Above Right: **Sunderland Flying Club Crest.** Hylton Castle above sextant.
Opposite Bottom: **Folland Gnat.** Entered service in 1962 and became the RAFs classic advanced jet trainer. It was extremely manoeuvrable which made it ideal as an aerobatic display aircraft. Previously in yellow as the 'YellowJacks'.

Above: **The Red Arrows.** The Usworth spot was one of many the team were doing on an aerobatic display tour of the whole country. Folland Gnats line up

Above: **Blackburn Beverley.** The RAFs short-haul heavy transport aircraft.

Above: **Squadron Aircraft Recognition Team.** Cpl Hall, Cadets Holyoak, Pattinson & Smith. Part of the 'Aircraft Knowledge' section of the syllabus. The team went on to win the Wing Aircraft 'Recce' Competition in 1968.

Above: Aircraft **Recognition Silhouettes.** Normally only one of the 3 views is shown, later develops into slideshows with photos from many angles. Classic 60's RAF fighters are English Electric Lightning (left) & Hawker Hunter (right)

Above: *AIRFIX* **Lightning & Hunter.** Making model kits has always been a good way of learning about aircraft for cadets - it's educational & fun (!)

Above Left: **Observers Book of Aircraft.** The classic text on learning the shapes. Progressing onto 'Janes' World Aircraft when pocket money would allow.
Above Right: **Air Cadet May'68.** The magazine tells of the coming of another British 'world first'- the Harrier 'jump jet' vertical takeoff & landing aircraft.

Above: **Traditional Modelling.** Balsa wood & dope still get an airing. *Left* Cadet Keith Loadman & *Right* Cadet Rob Norman.

Above Left: **Wartime Observer Corps Post.** Formed in 1925 the Observer Corps played its part in the Battle of Britain by giving the ID & numbers of enemy aircraft. For sterling service it was given the prefix 'Royal' in 1941.

Above Right: **Leaflets.** The role changed in the 50/60's to a nuclear reporting action due to the 'Cold War' between world powers. Leaflets explained how to be 'As safe as possible' (?) during a nuclear attack. Also the reasons for civil defence measures and organisations such as the ROC. Nuclear War threats.

The secondary role of aircraft recognition was still part of initial training, these skills were kept up to date with competitions as well as the 'Recognition Journal' issued to units. Also sent to cadet units via the RAF - 'Restricted'.

The local ROC monitoring post was at Springwell, adjacent the coal mine - north of Washington, regional control being at Durham.

In 1991 there was a partial stand-down due to easing world tensions. Eventually, in 1995, the corps was disbanded. Their loss was 2214's gain, as some Ex-members of ROC became Civilian Instructor staff members. Henceforth on squadron ROC became known as 'Macbeth'.

Above: **ROC Crest.**   **Recognition Journal.**   **The Manual.**

Above Left: **Ernie Guy at Springwell Post N4.** Coal mine in background.
Above Right: **Access.** Tommy Cairns descends to the post - a tight fit.

 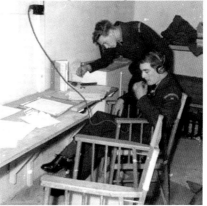

Above: **Post N4.** Access hatch & monitoring post below - communications.
Below: **Monitoring Post.** Cutaway & Diagram. Not much room inside.

 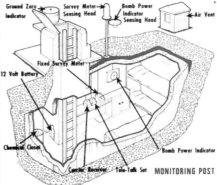

AIRDAY 68

SUNDERLAND AIRPORT

Above: **P51 Mustang.** The star of the show. It featured in the film 'The Mercenaries' released that year, starring Rod Taylor & Kenneth More.

Above: **Hawker Hunter MkF6.** Pilot Fg Off. Paul Day came from Sunderland.
Opposite Right: **EE Lightning.** Its power zoom climb into the clouds was a wonder to see and convinced the author to join the Air Cadets at Usworth.

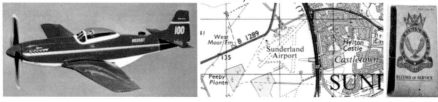

Above: **Jet Provost 'Gin Team'** Note the 3 Horse Shoes Pub in background.

1.45 p.m.	Opening Address by the Mayor of Sunderland
2.00 p.m.	Fly-Past.
2.15 p.m.	Bolkow & Victa Display. Sunderland Flying Club.
2.25 p.m.	Beagle 206.
2.30 p.m.	Currie Wot.
2.40 p.m.	Newcastle Flying Club Demonstration.
2.50 p.m.	Free Fall Parachute Drop. (Northumbria Parachute
3.00 p.m.	Stampe Aerobatic Display.
3.10 p.m.	Hovercraft demonstration.
3.20 p.m.	Set Piece (C.B. Bombing Etc.)
3.30 p.m.	Gyocopter demonstration.
3.40 p.m.	Mooney Ranger.
3.50 p.m.	R.F. 4 Display.
4.00 p.m.	Rogers Display. Cessna 337
4.10 p.m.	Mustang.
4.20 p.m.	Chipmunk - Solo Aerobatics.
4.30 p.m.	Helicopter Search and Rescue Demonstration.
4.40 p.m.	Hunters Fly-Past.
4.50 p.m.	Hunter Solo Aerobatics.
5.0 p.m.	Gin Team (Jet Provosts)
5.10 p.m.	Lightning Solo Aerobatics.

**SUNDERLAND FLYING CLUB
PRESENT AIRDAY '68
PROGRAMME OF EVENTS**

59

Above Left: **Chipmunk Flight**: Northumberland University Air Sqn flypast.
Above Right: **Freefall Parachuting**: Northumbria Parachute Club.

60

Above: **Air Day '67.** The size of the Beverley (P53) can be seen here, with Sopwith Pup (L) & Spitfire (R) Lamella hanger can be seen in the distance.

Above: **Andover (L) & Chipmunk (R).** Control tower in the background 1967.

Above Left: **Flt Lt Bob Jones.** Became 2214 Squadron CO in 1969. Flt Lt Joe Taylor retired having received the Cadet Forces Medal for 12 years service.
Above Right: **Air Day 1969.** Air days continued annually until the 1980's.

AIRFIX - 72 SCALE
LUNAR MODULE

Above: AIRFIX **Man on the Moon 1969.** July saw the first moon landing with *AIRFIX* responding with the appropriate model kit. Sans Command Module.

Left: Comet Ikeya-Seki photographed at the Boyden Observatory in Africa.

Centre: Craters on the Moon.

Bottom: A remote star system or galaxy made up of millions of suns.

THE BACKGROUND
OF ASTRONOMY

By PATRICK MOORE

We are living in the Space Age. Everyone nowadays must take at least a passing interest in astronomy; it has become part of our lives, and we read regularly of astronauts, rockets to the Moon and probes to the planets. Yet astronomy itself is the oldest of all sciences, and it dates back to the days when men lived in caves and gazed up at the skies.

It is also, of course, the basis of all timekeeping and navigation. Without astronomical methods there would be no good maps, and certainly no good navigators. Astro-navigation may not be used in the air so extensively as it used to be before and during the War, but its principles hold good, and we would be lost

astronomers prefer to use the light-year. This is the distance travelled by a ray of light in one year; it works out at rather less than 6 million million miles. The nearest star, excluding the Sun, is 4.3 light-years away.

The Sun is the centre of a family of nine planets, of which the Earth comes third in order of distance. Mercury, Venus, Mars, Jupiter and Saturn have been known since ancient times, because they are visible to the naked eye, and indeed Venus, Mars and Jupiter outshine any star. The three outer planets (Uranus, Neptune and Pluto) are of relatively modern detection; they were found in 1781, 1846 and 1930 respectively.

Occasionally the Moon may pass exactly between the Sun and the Earth. When this happens it blocks out the brilliant solar disc, and produces what is called an eclipse of the Sun. The effect is truly magnificent, because if the eclipse is total the Moon appears just large enough to hide the Sun completely, and for a few minutes we see the brilliant solar atmosphere or 'corona'. It is a pity that total eclipses do not happen more often. Stay in England, and you must wait until 1999; but there is a total eclipse to be seen this coming September—provided that you do not mind making a trip to Siberia!

Above: **Patrick Moore.** (Ex-ATC) had a regular spot in Air Cadet magazine.

AIR CADET
TRAINING HANDBOOK

BOOK 9

SPACE TRAVEL

Above: **Sunderland Rail Station 1969.** Not quite off to the moon - but it could be a different planet for some cadets. Usworth Squadron - 30 (!) cadets about to embark for summer camp at RAF Fairford, accommodated at South Cerney.

Above: **Venture Adventure.** CI Harry Hogarth with cadets from 2214. Cadet third left is a very young Colin Crann destined to become an AWO, then Squadron Leader on Wing Staff with a particular interest in shooting activities *Opposite Below:* **Lost in Space.** Cadet handbook did not land until *much* later.

Above: **Battle of Britain Fighters.** Squadron poses in front of a Spitfire (L) and (R) Messerschmitt 109. Flt Lt Jones kneeling (L) with PO Horsley (R) CI Harry Hogarth far left & the author directly above CO (back row). Cadets from L - Cdt Rob Norman, Clark, Swallow, Bailey, Brown, Johnson, (?), Paxman, Abbas, Yarnell, Author, (?), English, (?), Bridge, (?), (?), Coulter, Loadman, Swallow, Mould, & Lee, RAF Fairford. Me109 now in RAF Hendon Museum.

Above: **'Herky Bird'.** In US speak but C130 Hercules with RAF. The pleasure of 'circuits & bumps' with rookie pilots for a few hours is memorable. Classic *AIRFIX* Roy Cross artwork showing a Bloodhound SAM with land rover being loaded onto a 'Transport Command' aircraft in desert colours.

Above: **RAF 'V' Bomber Base Classics.** Avro Vulcan & Bloodhound SAM.

RAF Fairford (South Cerney) 1969

L-R **Front:** 2nd Colin Lee, 3rd AWO Routledge, 4th F/O Sid Close, 5th Flt Lt Bob Jones, 6th Wg Cdr Gowing, 9th CI Harry Hogarth, 10th Sgt Chapman, 11th Cpl Denis Lee. **Middle:** Cpl Kevin Henderson, Phil Coulter, 4th Colin Swallow, 8th Colin Crann, 10th Jim Clark, 13th Cpl Colin Bailey. **Back:** John English, Reggie Bridge, 5th Jim Yarnell, 6th Keith Loadman, 9th Devine, 12th Author. (Although camp listed as Fairford was billited at South Cerney)

65

Above: **VC10.** Another Transport Command aircraft used for cadet air experience flying at the 1969 camp. Alas not for the cadet author - who lost on a draw for seats and spent the afternoon tenpin bowling.

Above: **RAF Stations.** South Cerney was camp base with Fairford for flying. Brize Norton & Lyneham being Transport Commands main stations..

ROYAL AIR FORCE

SWIMMING PROFICIENCY CERTIFICATE

This is to certify that   CADET WALMSLEY   NO.2214 SQUADRON ATC

on   18th AUGUST   19 69 , at   CIRENCESTER BATHS

attained the following standards in swimming:

Swam 150 yards continuously using the following strokes for 50 yards each:
  i. *Breast stroke.*
  ii. *Back stroke and*
  iii. *Free style (other than (i.) or (ii.)).*

for AIR COMMODORE
AIR *Officer Commanding*   HQ AIR CADETS
RAF BRAMPTON

Sqn Ldr

Above L: **In the Swim.** Typical of qualifications gained at camp, a swimming certificate from Cirencester *open-air* (!) baths. Freezing at 9.30am.

Above: **Concorde.** The British version 002 was based at RAF Fairford in Gloucestershire. This was a visit as part of the summer camp. Cadets got to view her close up. It first flew in April 1969, the camp was in August.

Above: **HRH Duke of Edinburgh & Brian Trubshaw in Concorde's Cockpit.** Cadets got to meet Brian - the test pilot & had a guided tour of the aircraft. He was also the test pilot for the VC10 (P66).   *Below:* **Anglo/French Meeting.**

5. <u>Commanding Officer's report</u>.

The enrolled strength of thensquadron is 62, with 28 probationers.
Recruiting was steady.

Summer Camp was held at RAF Fairford. The CO with F/O Close and
Mr. Hoggarth CI attended with 30 cadets. Excellent flying in VC
10, Hercules, and Belfast aircraft was enjoyed. It was regretted
 that owing to an engine change the Concord was not seen flying.
A film of the camp's activities was made and would be shown at
some later date.

Above: **Minute Book.** Section from Civilian Committee Book. Note squadron strength with 28(!) probationer cadets, which would lead to additional accommodation. Also note Concorde's engine change - who knows we might have been able to take it up for a spin - would have been a noteworthy addition to the flying log. If anyone knows the location of the said 'film of activities' please contact the squadron - we can turn super 8 into a DVD.

Year 1969		AIRCRAFT		Captain or 1st Pilot	Co-pilot 2nd Pilot Pupil or Crew	DUTY (Including number of day or night landings as 1st Pilot or Dual)
Month	Date	Type and Mark	No.			
—	—	—	—	—		— Totals brought forward
APRIL	1	BEAGLE	GAVITO	SELF		Filton - Wisley
APRIL	2	HERON	GANNO	SELF		Wisley - Filton
APRIL	3	HERON	GANNO	SELF		Wisley - Filton
APRIL	9	CONCORDE	G-BSST	SELF	CREW	1st Flight. 002
						Wisley to Filton - Return

Above: **Flying Log.** Excerpt from Brian Trubshaw's flying log showing the first flight of Concorde 002 on 9th April 1969. Only a matter of weeks before the cadets of 2214 cast their envious eyes over her sleek delta design framework.

Air Cadet May '69   **RAF Yearbook 1969**   **Royal Mail Stamp**

Fairey Delta 2. Broke the world speed record in 1956 at 1,132MPH. An all British thin-winged delta, it had a pioneering 'Droop Snoot' nose design that was later incorporated into the Concorde. Never went into production.

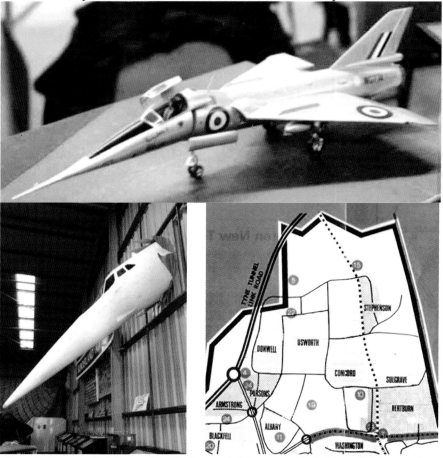

Above L: **Concorde Nose. -** Breaks through Hanger end at Aircraft Museum!
Above R: **Concord.** is a named district of Washington (UK) Tyne & Wear.

Above: **Battle of Britain Film 1969.**   **RAF Usworth 1940's Map.**

Above: **Maps: Correct Course.**   **Navigational Error.**

There is a short 5 minute sequence in the film depicting the 15th August attack from Norway (P16). Scenes show (L) correct course that should have been taken & (R) the actual track. Spitfires are shown attacking HE 111s, this was 72 Sqn from Acklington, Northumberland. RAF Usworth 607 Sqn attacked off Newcastle/Sunderland with 41 Sqn finally joining in from Catterick. The ME 110's were not shown as there were no flying examples available. **72Sqn Spit.**

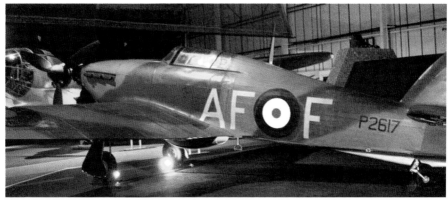

Above: **RAF Museum Hendon London.** The 'Battle of Britain' hall houses Blackadder's 607 Squadron Hawker Hurricane in AF-F codes. In front a rather appropriate HE 111 German bomber of the type shot down by Blackadder. In 1951 his aircraft was also one of the 'stars' in the film *'Angels One Five'*.

Flt Lt Blackadder.   **Fg Off Ben Benions** then & now.   **DVD.**

Ben flew 41Sqn Spitfires from Catterick & got an Me110 over Barnard Castle.

Above: **Battle of Britain Commemorative Stamps 1969.**

Below: **Aircraft Recognition.** How many can you identify?

FOUR

1970'S

Above: **RAF F4 Phantom, 111 Squadron, RAF Leuchars.** Signed print by squadron pilots from a summer camp, mounted in squadron conference room.

Above: **RAF Recruiting Booklet.**   *Above:* **ATC Recruiting Poster.**

Above: **'Cadets Shown the Latest Weapons'.** - Sunderland Echo, Feb 1970.

Army and Air Cadets joined forces last night when a demonstration team from the 1st Bn. Royal Anglian Regiment, Catterick, gave a talk and demonstrated modern weapons in use by the Regular Army to members of the Usworth squadron A.T.C. and the Washington detachment of the Army Cadet Force, Durham, in the A.T.C. headquarters.

The team is visiting Army and Air Cadet Forces throughout the county.

Above: Air Cadet Derek Brown (13), of High Row, Washington (left) and David Gonzales (13) of the Washington detachment of the A.C.F., Durham, hold a Carl Gustav anti-tank gun while Pte Harry Gibson of the 1st Bn. Royal Anglian Regiment, Catterick, explains in detail how the gun operates.

Right: Senior Air Cadet John English (15), of Manor Park, Washington (left) aims a general purpose machine-gun assisted by 14-year-old Tony O'Brien, of Station Road, Washington, a member of the Washington detachment of the Army Cadet Force, Durham. —S.E.

An example of inter-services co-operation in action. The RAF Regiment would probably be the choice for ATC cadets.

Above: **'The Country Code'.** - Lecture presentation by the newly commissioned Pilot Officer Horsley. He was responsible for Adventure Training & the 'DofE' Duke of Edinburgh's Award training. Note 70's technology - chalk & blackboard. Skills were practically tested on map reading exercises outdoors.

Above: "**So - *You* Want to be an Air Cadet?**". - The caption that went with this picture. F/O Sid Close interviews a prospective recruit. Note battledress/wings

Leading Cadet Certificate.   **Basic/Leading Badge(Bottom)**   'Little Nellie'

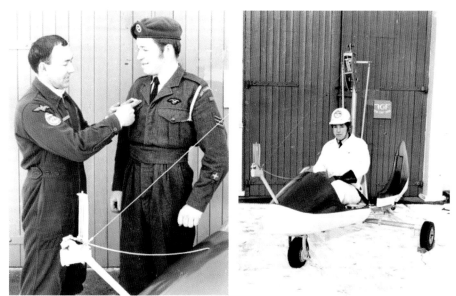

Above: **Gyroglider Wings.** Sergeant Denis Lee receives his wings as a qualified gyroglider pilot. A sponsored private venture similar to gliding & flying scholarships. Note similarity to James Bond's 'Little Nellie' autogyro featured in the film *'You Only Live Twice'* (1967). Minus guns & missiles of course.

Below: **Battle of Britain Parade.** Colour Party with .303 Rifles, Sunderland.

Above: **RAF Wattisham - Lightning Country.** Annual Camp August 1970 features 111 Squadron Lightnings. A week of aircraft heaven for that cadet who joined on seeing the one that flew at the Usworth 1968 Air Day (P59).

Above: **RAF Wattisham.** - Adjacent Ipswich in Suffolk. 111 Squadron went on to convert to the 'new' American F4 Phantom later in the 1970's.

Above L: **AIRFIX** **Catalogue.** Features early 111 Squadron Lightnings.
Above R: **111 Squadron Crest.** The 'tremblers' in 2214 Conference Room.

Air Training Corps.

Certificate of Training

This is to Certify that

Cadet   D. WALMSLEY
of No.   27th (Usworth)   Squadron
has qualified as a Senior Cadet by
obtaining a   Credit
in the Senior Cadet Examination

Commandant.
Air Training Corps.

Dated this 28th day of   May   19 70

Above Left: **RAF Wattisham Squadron Efficiency Shield.** For the first time Usworth Squadron won the Efficiency Shield. An accumulation of points won over the week on everything from tactical exercises to block tidiness.

Above Right: **Senior Cadet Certificate.** - A Credit no less.

Above Left: **Lightning Art - Conference Room.** Oil painting of a Lightning above the pitot tube of the real thing (!) - (cover was left on whilst heating).

Above Right: **Senior Cadet Badge.**

Above: **Presentation Night.** Cadets receive awards/certificates at the annual award ceremony. Wing Commander R. Gowing CO of Durham Wing presents the trophies. Note Squadron efficiency shield from the RAF Wattisham summer camp (left of cricket bat). CO Flt Lt Jones to right of Wing Co.

Wing Commander R. Gowing, Commanding Officer of the Durham Wing, Air Training Corps, is pictured (above) with members of 2214 (Usworth) Squadron, A.T.C., when he presented awards to members at the squadron's headquarters last night.

After an efficiency plaque won by the squadron while at summer camp at R.A.F. Wattisham, was received by Flight-Sgt. Colin Lee, Wing Commander Gowing presented individual awards.

The Richard Thompson Trophy, for the best all-round cadet over the past year, went to Sgt. Kevin Henderson, who is joining the R.A.F. this month. The Taylor Trophy, for the most efficient N.C.O., was presented to Flight-Sgt. Lee.

Sgt. James Clarke, who was elected "Sportsman of the Year," was presented with a cricket bat. He is pictured here with Wing Commander Gowing.

James, aged 15, of Coach Road Estate, Washington, is a pupil of Usworth Comprehensive School, and has been a member of the Usworth squadron for three years.

Above: **'Night of Awards for Usworth ATC Cadets'.** Sunderland Echo report on proceedings. Sept 1970.

Above: '**Focus on Usworth ATC'.** Sunderland Echo covers project work.

Photography plays an important part in project training for these members of Usworth A.T.C. who meet at their headquarters in Washington Road on Tuesday and Thursday evenings. Left to right are: **Cpl. John English (16),** of Albany Village, **Sgt. Jim Clarke (15),** of Coach Road Estate, and **Sgt. Colin Bailey,** of Campbell Road, Hylton Castle Estate, Sunderland.

With the aid of CI's this involved taking & then developing(!) black & white photographs with the aid of a darkroom and many assorted noxious chemicals. All done at the squadron HQ. *Below:* More Awards.

L-Cdt Rob Norman holds Richard Thompson Cup for 'Best All Round Cadet'.

Above: **Avro Vulcan V-Bomber XM610.** In happier times on takeoff at RAF Wildenrath in Germany. Later to crash at Wingate, County Durham, Jan 1971.

10. 1. 71. A party of Cadets accompanied by the C.O Flt/Lt. R.E. Jones assisted the R.G.F in clearing the wreckage of the VULCAN which crashed at Wingate.

Above & Opposite: **Reporting : Squadron Logbook Entry & Sunderland Echo.**
Vulcan XM610 got into difficulties due to an engine fire which spread to adjacent engine and wing/fuel tanks. This was later found to be due to a detached turbine blade. The pilot Flt Lt Robert Alcock was awarded the Air Force Cross & the crew the Queens Commendation for 'valuable service in the air'. It past low over a school before crashing in a field behind the CO-OP. Gary Foreman, a serving fire fighter at Farringdon Stn, Tyne & Wear, saw the incident - he was aged 11, at the RC Junior School: "We saw the plane from the playground, it came down very low before hearing a tremendous noise and seeing a large black mushroom cloud appear behind the houses. The teachers then took us inside and we all prayed that no-one had been hurt."
Below: **A Possible Crash Site Scene.** Cadets clearing wreckage - more likely a 'FOD' sweep to collect pieces/paperwork.(Health & Safety arrives in 1974(!))

HUNT FOR V-BOMBER WRECKAGE

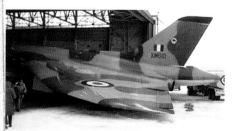

MEMBERS of the 2214 Usworth Squadron of the A.T.C. at Sunderland went to Wingate yesterday to help a R.A.F. team in the search for, and clearance of, wreckage of the Vulcan bomber which crashed near the village on Friday.

Fourteen cadets, led by the squadron commander, Flight-Lieutenant R. E. Jones, went to Wingate at the request of the R.A.F., and cleared three fields of scattered wreckage.

DOCUMENTS

Dozens of documents from the crashed bomber have been handed in at Peterlee police station.

Pieces, some of them quite large, from the aircraft, which caught fire while on a routine training flight, are also being handed in. It is all being handed over to the R.A.F. and the investigation into the near-disaster — led by six specialists in crash probes — is continuing.

Chief Supt. H. Marsden reports that numerous documents, flight plans and maps have been recovered. "Dozens of items have been handed in by the public, who are co-operating to the fullest extent," he said.

***Flt Lt Jim Vinale the Nav Plotter in the crew of this aircraft - who all safely bailed out over Rothbury in Northumberland - will appear later in our story in the 1980's with (strangely enough) another Vulcan's final flight.

Above: **AFC Air Force Cross.** Flt Lt Alcock awarded for 'Valuable Service'.

Above: **New Hut Opening Parade 1971.** Squadron Compound. Group Captain & Wg Cdr Gowing inspect Cpls Crann (Ctr) & Loadman (2nd R) & Sgt Clark.

Above L: **Parade Inspection.** Note former airport building in background.
Above R: **Keys to the Door.** Gp Cap turns the key while CO does the honours
Opposite: **Opening Ceremony.** Official party poses for the camera, CO 4th L.

Above: **Gliding RAF Catterick.** Cadet Cpl Bailey with CO of gliding school Flt Lt K. Hall seated in a Sedbergh T21 glider. Note aircraft in the distance - hulks used by the RAF Fire Service School for training purposes - Javelin/Valetta?

Above: **Gliding RAF Catterick.** Kirby Cadet Mk3 tandem seat glider ready for winch launch. Note Handley Page Hastings in the background.

RAF Catterick Crest.   RAF Firefighting School Crest.

Above L: AIRFIX **Harrier GR1.** Lightning, Hercules and Spitfire in box out.
Above R: **Cadet Glider Cockpit.** Not a lot in the way of instrumentation

Above: **Silver Duke of Edinburgh's Award Presentations.** Above L sees RAF Craft Apprentice Kevin Henderson (17) former squadron cadet receive his award from CO Flt Lt Bob Jones. Now a regular airman based at RAF Halton. Above R has Sqn Ldr J. Flemming of RAF Topcliffe presenting the award to Flt Sgt Colin Lee (17) an apprentice fitter at Coles Cranes in Sunderland.

Above: **Duke of Edinburgh's Award Badges.** The award has Bronze, Silver & Gold standards. An add on then - now part of cadet curriculum. / **News 1978.**

LEARNING ABOUT LIFE UP IN THE AIR

Cadets of Usworth Squadron Air Training Corps undergo instruction in various subjects that will help them if they make their career in the RAF. Here some of them are seen at work and at play.

Quenching a pint sized thirst are (left) Cadets Peter Brown (14), of Bergen St and Andrew Mcginley (13), of Seaview Rd. Looking after the canteen are ex-members of the now defunct Girls Venture Corps, Mary Wilson and Jacqueline Haddock.

Fourteen year old Stephen Tye, of Hylton Castle, Sunderland, during a radio training operation with instructor John Wollage of Watford Close. With them are Colin Crann (16) Radlett Road, and Colin Bailey (18) all of Sunderland.

89

Above: **RAF Waddington Annual Camp 1973.** CO Bob Jones with a group of (rather small) squadron cadets, behind is an Avro Lancaster WW2 bomber.

Above: *AIRFIX* **Avro Lancaster.** Classic Roy Cross artwork. Note the new *Airfix* 'roundel' type logo replacing banner type. 'G for George' returns home.

The Cadets also witnessed the arrival at Ouston of the SPITFIRE from the Historic A/c Flight - prepartion for a display at R.A.F Boulmer on the 15th. This day also saw the last flying done by No. 11. A.E.F before transfering to R.A.F LEEMING, on the CLOSURE OF OUSTON. A sad day for all! The arrival of the SPITFIRE was a fitting moment!

Above: **Squadron Log 14th Sept 1974.** RAF Ouston closes with 11 AEF moving to RAF Leeming in Yorkshire. A Spitfire flypast is a fitting tribute, as 607 County of Durham Sqn (P16) flew F22 Griffin engined Spitfires from there in 1948. Note Sqn Griffin crest on nose & No 4 marking for Cooper Trophy Race.

Above: **Princess Ann Royal Flight 1974.** Princess flies in to Sunderland Airport to open the Galleries shopping centre at Washington. Aircraft is a special Andover of the Royal Flight - note standard above cockpit & 'E-R' on nose.

Above: **Exiting Airport/Tour.** Royal car drives through exit enroute to Galleries centre - note Lamella hanger to left of photograph. Crowds at town centre.

Above: **AIRFIX** BAC Jaguar 1974. *Below:* **AIRFIX** Hawker Harrier.

Above: **Roy Cross, Artist.** 1974 was the year Roy retired from creating *AIRFIX* box top art. No doubt he also created many model sales with his inspiring action packed memorable scenes. Many Ex cadets salute you sir in providing the gateway to an enjoyable hobby. With a little help from *AIRFIX* of course.

93

Above: **A Hurricane Returns to Usworth.** A memorable appearance at the 1973 AirDay recalls the glory days of 607 Sqn in the Battle of Britain 1940 (P17/70).

Above L: **Flt Lt Sid Close.** New 2214 CO from 1977 takes over from Bob Jones.
Above R: **RAF Buccaneer.** Being pulled out of the Lamella hanger at Usworth after having to make an unscheduled landing (bird strike). The American exchange pilot thought Sunderland Airport was Newcastle(!)

Above: **RAF Scampton Annual Camp 1977.** New CO Sid Close far left with AWO Cummings kneeling at front right. Lancaster bomber to rear of group.
Below: **NEAM Arrives at Sunderland Airport 1977.** Cadets get to work cleaning a Danish Hunter for the newly arrived North East Aircraft Museum. *Opposite Bottom*: Hunter location outside Lamella hanger and NEAM logo showing a Sunderland Flying Boat indicating museum location. Eventually would have to move again - over the road to make way for Nissan car plant.

Above: **Tiger Moth Rally at Usworth 1979.** June sees the arrival of numerous Tiger Moths to mark the 50th anniversary of the Gipsy Reliability Tour of 1929. Another Déjà-Vu for Usworth as Moths used to fly from here. Note famous landmark Penshaw Monument to the right of photo in the distance.

Below: **Prize Draw.** Cadets & staff wait to see if they could be a winner. Note Lamella hanger in centre of photo with control tower to left behind group. Cadets would assist in marshalling, crowd control and programme selling.

Below: Yellow Moth in front of the hangers at Usworth.(with dummy pilot)

Above: **Plastic Model Making.** Visiting officer admires handy work of cadet enthusiasts. Note *AIRFIX* 1/24th scale Spitfire box and Apollo 11 spacecraft. Probably being made for entry into Wing competitions which later included diorama settings. Also note officer's 'polo mint' brevet just above medal ribbons- Observer, - an increasingly rare attainment in the RAF.

Above: **Battle of Britain Memorial Flight Spitfire at Usworth.** The real thing appeared at both 1979 & 80 Air Days. Note Usworth's Lamella hanger in the background with part of callendar hanger at far left.

Above: **Church Parade.** Cadet colour party at Durham Wing Chaplains church
- St Margaret's of Castletown Sunderland, back to squadron roots.

Above: **Tornado *Low*.** F3 Tornado of 11 Squadron makes a *very* low pass over RAF Leeming in full afterburner. 23 & 25 squadrons joined it in making the Tornado Air Defence Wing. Hawk trainers of 100 squadron completing units.

Above: **Sqn Staff.** L-R CI Stan Miller, Plt Off Stan Hardwick, CI Benson Adams

Above: **RAF Waddington Annual Camp 1980.** AWO Alan Cummings far right.

Above: '**Vintage Pair**'. Meteor & Vampire appeared at the final Air Day 1981.

Above Left: **The LAST Air Day 1981.** Note Fairey Delta2 (Btm-L) from page 69.
Above Right: **Flt Lt Derek Crozier.** New 2214 CO from 1981, takes over from
Sid Close and brings a historic icon from the RAF to the squadron compound.

Above: **RAF Leeming Annual Camp 1981.** Javelin 'Flat Iron' gate guardian.

Above Left: **ATC Recruiting Poster 1980s** Girls are allowed to join the ATC with the arrival of the 80s. 'Battledress' has finally given way to the 'Wooley Pulley' standard NATO jumper. The Chipmunk is still flying though. (& SLR).

Above Right: **Durham Northumberland Wing Crest.** 1981 sees the amalgamation of Durham (Usworths Wing) & Northumberland Wings during reorganisation. Wg Cdr Harry Lowe OBE became its first CO, he went on to become the longest serving Wing Commander in the history of the ATC.

Last flights

Whilst on a visit to Leeming, one of the members of staff of 2214 (Usworth) Sqn saw a Vampire T.11 standing on a dump ready for burning. He approached Wg Cdr

Hobbs (OC Engineering), who spoke to the station commander and it was agreed that the squadron could have it, if they dismantled the aircraft and provided transport to remove it.

It was dismantled in only two days, and Wg Cdr Hobbs was so pleased with the speed of the operation, that he offered transport.

At Usworth the aircraft parts were lifted and placed into the squadron compound by Coles Cranes, a Sunderland crane manufacturer.

The aircraft is now assembled and is in the process of being refurbished. The squadron will be using the aircraft to teach airframes, and construction.

Above: **Vampire Gate Guardian XD622.** Squadron compound 1981 with CI Larry Little posing in front of the assembled / refitted aircraft.

Above: **Vampire FB Mk9 607 County of Durham Squadron.** 607 Sqn flew Vampires from RAF Ouston in 1956 when they moved from RAF Usworth. It is therefore fitting that an aircraft of this type still stands guard over 2214.

Opposite: **Vampire Lift.** Air Cadet News covers the Vampire story. Note condition of aircraft on crane & amount of work required assemble / finish. Construction under supervision of CIs F. Dart & Stan Miller. Delivery scenes were to be repeated in 2001 with a very different aircraft on guard.

Above: **Squadron Photo Call.** An impromptu shot sees cadets formed up in the main hall in front of posters of various RAF 80s aircraft.

Above: **Vulcan XL319 Landing at Usworth 1983.** A notable date for Usworth sees the Vulcan V-Bomber being added to the NEAM (North East Aircraft Museum) collection. Part of the crew was Flt Lt Jim Vinale the Nav Plotter of the Wingate crash Vulcan from Page 83, Sqn Ldr MacDougall piloting. The Falklands Crisis of 1982 had delayed delivery due to operational commitment.

Above: **Vulcan Standing** A couple of young aircraft enthusiasts pose in front of the new arrival. To the left of picture just below the wing is Penshaw Monument in the distance - fixing location still on Airport site at Usworth. This aircraft will appear later in our story & helps to increase squadron funds.

Above: **Nissan.** 15.00hrs 31st May 1984 sees the end of all flying activities at Usworth. Sunderland Airport is sold off to make way for the Nissan Motor Co. The 1929 Lamella hanger can be seen to the right of the sign - kept for storage, RAF sends a Jet Provost to flypast to mark the occasion. NEAM is relocated over the road to the north side of the complex.

Opposite Bottom: **NEAM Re-Located.** Aerial shot showing complex North of Washington Road. 2214 HQ can be seen in top left corner with two huts & Vampire guard. Vulcan is in bottom right corner, Varsity at centre + hangers.

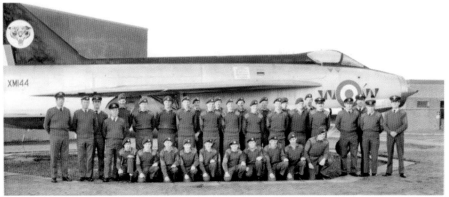

Above: **RAF Leuchars Annual Camp 1986.** EE Lightning in background.

Above: **Chipmunk AEF at RAF Leeming.** Note 11 AEF crest on nose & control tower of Leeming at far left. Now based in Yorkshire after Northumberland. The 'Chippy' soldiers on, and will not be replaced in AEF units until 1996 - by the Scottish Aviation Bulldog. Plenty still flying about today though.

Above: **RAF Church Fenton Annual Camp 1988.** Tucano training aircraft in background. Plt Off Stan Hardwick is 4th from right in the front row.

Above: **Typhoon Takes to the Skies.** 11 (Ex-Leeming) Sqn updates kit.

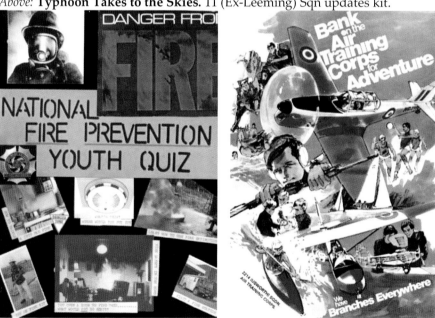

Above Left: **Fire Quiz.** Cadets from 2214 got through to the regional final of the Tyne & Wear Fire Brigade competition. They also got to wear fire kit, visit fire stations & put out real fires using various extinguishers during training.

Above Right: **Recruit Poster.** The Chipmunk still takes centre stage promoting flying, other activities detail the 'adventure' of the corps motto.

Above: **Golden Celebration 1991.** ATC notes passing of 50 years since formation in 1941. Many events are held nationwide, see Usworth's opposite.

Above L: **RAF Yearbook 1991.** Featuring Jaguars from the Gulf War in desert colours. Concorde is still flying - with the chance of winning a supersonic seat.
Above R: **WISE CRACK- 1st Squadron Magazine.** Cadets with the assistance of CI John Killick go into desktop publishing & reporting. Editor is Cadet M. Brown, modelling editor G. Edminson & reporter M. Phillips. A monthly periodical of six pages. Interviewed CO is Flt Lt Derek Crozier.

75. A significant landmark in ATC history came in 1991 with the Corps' Golden Glider Jubilee. The initial launch of the 50th Anniversary year took place on 31 January 1991 at the Southampton Hall of Aviation when the AOC Air Cadets, Air Commodore Skelley, received the Air League Challenge Cup from Mr Michael Cobham, chairman of the Air League. The cup was awarded to the Corps in recognition of the outstanding contribution made to British aviation over the past 50 years. A Service of Thanksgiving was held on 3rd February at the Central Church of the RAF, St Clement Danes, in the presence of HRH the Duke of Edinburgh.

76. Some events that took place to celebrate the 50th Anniversary of the Corps include:

a. Burton-on-Trent's local County Council prepared the ATC crest in flowers in gardens situated near the town centre.

b. 195 (Grimsby) Sqn presented their local church with 5 kneelers, all made by the cadets. Each kneeler represented 10 years of the ATC and bearing the Grimsby Coat of Arms.

c .2214 (Usworth) Sqn constructed a raised garden for the residents of a local nursing home.

d. West Mercian Wing commissioned an embroidered panel depicting the Wing area and Corps activities and presented it to the Aerospace Museum at RAF Cosford.

e. East Essex Wing took 20 cadets, 9 Mountain Instructors and a logistics team of 3 to link with 504 (Montgomery) Sqn Royal Canadian Air Cadets for an expedition in the Rocky Mountains.

31.1.1-22

Above L: **50th Anniversary Garden Project 1991.** Back L CWO Karl Shovlin, Back R CWO Dave Mann, Front L Cdt Alan Mason, Centre Cdt Paul Adgar. R Cdt Jamie Murray. Constructed over a series of weeks the completed project enabled home residents to participate in gardening at a convenient height.
Above R: **Cadet Training Manual: The ATC.** Page from the history section detailing 50th events - 2214's highlighted at 'C' - Raised Garden Project.

Above: **RAF Lossiemouth Annual Camp 1993.** Buccaneer aircraft as backdrop. Far L CWO Dave Mann, Far R Flt Lt Brian Adgar, to his R CI Benson Adams. Nose art depicts the 'Sea Witch' - Debbie, appeared in the Gulf War when these craft were used for laser target designation pending Tornado arrival.

Above: **Kielder Camp 1991.** Adventure training camp at Hawkhurst, DofE prep. From L CI's Mrs Mason, Author, Mr Killick, Centre Flt Lt Adgar. Note base camp flag & tents to right, woods are part of Kielder Forest Nat. Park.

Above Left: **Flt Lt Brian Adgar.** New 2214 CO from 1993, takes over from Derek Crozier - who 'retires' but goes on to a place on the civilian committee.
Above Right: **Worral Trophy Presentation.** Wing Commander Worral (Rtd) presents Aircraftsman John Carrington (previously Cdt) with cup for highest attainment in cadet examinations. He was also the winner of the Currall Trophy - a national award given for academic achievement.

Above: **Squadron Parade.** CWO Metcalf takes the parade in the compound. Note 'Basics' Flt to right, NEAM hanger to rear & Vampire to right.

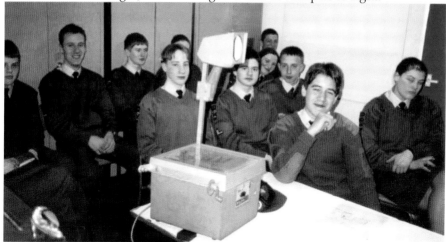

Above: **Class Hi-Tec.** Squadron advances with the use of overhead projectors as aids to teaching. Cdt Scott Harrison (3rd L) goes on to become a CI at 2214.

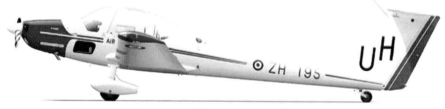

Above: **Vigilant.** Grob 109 motor gliders are introduced from the 1990's.

Above: **Vulcan Wash 1995.** The biggest squadron 'Project' sees cadets clean the 'Old Lady' of NEAM - the very same aircraft that landed in 1993 (p104).

Above: **Mop & Bucket Brigade.** Cadets apply the elbow grease required.

CADETS GIVE OLD LADY A SPONGE DOWN FOR CASH!

Cadets from 2214 (Usworth) Squadron are all washed up — after making a big splash for squadron funds.

Armed with mops and sponges, some 40 cadets offered to wash an Avro Vulcan Bomber belonging to the local North East Aircraft Museum.

Vulcan B2XL319 (nicknamed 'The Old Lady' by Museum staff), formerly with 617 and 83 Squadrons at RAF Scampton and 44 Squadron at RAF Waddington, was flown to Sunderland on 21 January 1983 and last saw soap and water in 1991!

After six weeks of planning the cadets began the mightly sponsored washathon — with 40 buckets and mops, 1,000 gallons of water, a fire engine, hydraulic platform, field kitchen and hard hats at their disposal.

Five hours of hard work scrubbing, mopping and hosing

Cadet Iain Edgar taking part in the sponsored clean up of 'The Old Lady' to raise funds for the Squadron. (The Sunderland Echo)

down later, 40 wet and weary cadets had succeeded in removing several years of accumulated dirt from 'The Old Lady', raised more than £500 for Squadron funds and left the North East Aircraft Museum's prize exhibit ready for this summer's visitors.

Above: **Air Cadet Report.** With Cdt Iain Adgar posing for the camera.

Above Left: **Hydraulic Platform.** Cadets clean tailfin with mops from cage.
Above Centre: **Air Cadet.** magazine front cover August 1995.
Opposite Right: **Everything Stops for Tea.** CO Flt Lt Adgar, Mrs Adgar & Committee Chairman Ernie Ross. Gill Air aircraft to left - NEAM HQ.
Opposite Left: **Hose Reel Washdown.** F/Sgt Edminson uses the fire appliance high pressure gun to wash off the last of the dirt from the underside.

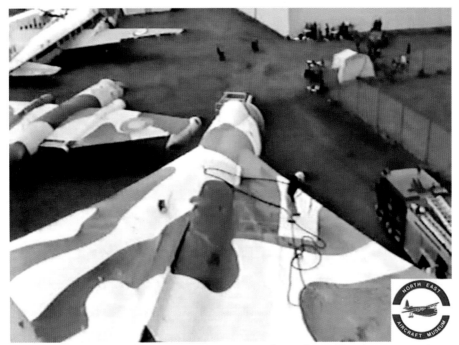

Above: **View from the Top.** HP provides view from the tailfin showing author untangling hose reel & Young Fire Fighter's fire appliance. Canberra to left with Valetta at top, destroyed by a fire in 1997. Cadet project HQ /mess at tent

Above: **Firebear.** Squadron sponsors Trauma Bear for use during road accidents involving children. Handover was covered by Tyne-Tees Television.

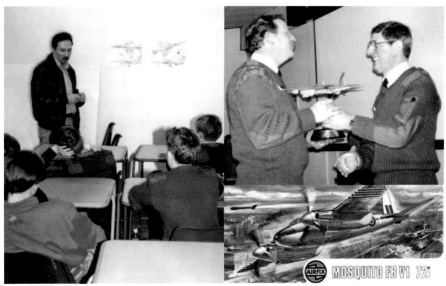

Above Left: **Aircraft Recognition.** Author details differences: F16 from MiG21.
Above Right: **Wing Aircraft Recognition Trophy Winners (X3).** The payoff for all that work. 2214 scores a hat-trick by winning the trophy 3 times in a row. Wing Commander Harry Lowe presents the Mosquito trophy to CO Flt Lt Brian Adgar. *Inset:* Design based on *AIRFIX* model but made of wood (natch)

Above: **Cadet 100 Marksman.** Cadet Sgt Ashish Raichura presented award at Bisley from AOC Air Cdre Jon Ford, Sgt went on to join RAF as an officer.

Above: **Tornado HAS Visit .** Cadets inspect an F3 during AEF turnaround.

Above: **S.A. Bulldog 11 AEF RAF Leeming** . In 1996 the Bulldog replaces the Chipmunk after completing 40 years service. Flt Lt Roy Turgoose pilot/CO

Above Left: **Bulldog Panel** . A poster for getting a handle on instruments.
Above Right: **Flight Kit.** Cadet models the latest flight suit & helmet.

Above: **RAF Lossiemouth Annual Camp 1996.** Buccaneer Déjà-Vu.

Above: **Lees Trophy Inspection 1998.** Group Captain Bill Gambold chats to cadets at Nissan complex CO to R CWO Michelle Craggs, & Plt Off Armstrong

Above: **Lees Trophy Honour Guard.** .303 rifles in Nissan compound.

Above: **Biggles Blaze Bear Flys Again 1999.** Another 'Trauma Ted' bear for Tyne & Wear Fire Service. This time complete with flying goggles, scarf, wings (of course) and that all important 2214 ID badge. Cadets: 3rd from L, Susan Carr, 4th L, Plt Off John Metcalf , Cdt Hughes & L/ff Joe Cummings.

Above: **Remembrance Day Parade 1999.** Cadets march down to Washington Village green en-route to parade. At war memorial cadets stand as honour guard, by this time .303 rifles have been withdrawn & policy is not to carry arms in public areas. Liaison is made with Royal British Legion for collections by cadets on behalf of the Poppy Appeal at supermarkets & town centre.

Above: **Lightning F35.** Future RAF fighter aircraft. (Name lives on from p78).
Below: **Phantom FGR2.** 2214 Squadron fighter aircraft (Gate Guardian) 2001.

Left: **60th Anniversary Logo.** Sticker celebrates another decade for ATC, 2001.
Centre: **Phantom Guard.** 56 Squadron fighter in Usworth's compound.
Right: **2214 Crest.** Squadron logo depicting original 80's Vampire gate guard.

Above: **Déjà-Vu & Flypast.** Phantom XV460 delivered. L- does a retake of p102 from the 80's. R- Flies over Vampire to sit opposite in squadron compound.

Above: **Squadron Band - Hylton Castle Millennium Festival 2000.** The castle that gave 'Castletown' Sqn its name (p22). Note 'leopard skin' tabards at right.

Above: **Déjà-Vu2 - Hylton Castle Millennium Festival.** The squadron 'van' - L, R - with a similar scene at Usworth(?) 60 years earlier? - Hurricane optional.

Above: **Grob Tutor 11AEF RAF Leeming.** The Tutor replaced the Bulldog in 1999 - built mainly of carbon fibre reinforced plastic, note NUAS crest on fin.

Above: **The Mile Wide Smile.** Chipmunk, Bulldog or Tutor, the kit may change but the result is the same- with a certificate to prove it. The Air in ATC

Above: **RAF Leuchars Annual Camp 2002.** Phantom at rear is appropriate, also a 43 Sqn (Fighting Cocks) machine. At one time the Sqn was based at RAF Usworth during the Battle of Britain, resting from the front line down south.

Above: **Warcop Greens Camp 2002.** Army base enroute to the Lake District.

Above: **L98 Marksman Training.**   *Above:* **Assault Course.**

Above: **DiY Rafting.** Good knots help keep it together, Venture Adventure.

Above: **'Arcadia' Battle Simulator.**   *Above:* **ARC: Plan of Attack/Leadership.**

122

Above: **Squadron Band-NEAM.** Queen's Diamond Jubilee celebrations+Vulcan

Above: **ARC: Control/Teambuilding.**   *Above:* **ARC: Tea & Medals (Edible).**

Above: **Dambusters 70th Project (FBW) at WHF.** *Above:* **Lancaster Project.**

Above: **Rotary Euphoniums.**   *Above:* **Dalek Project at WHF.**   Festival

Above: **2214 (USWORTH) Squadron HQ at Dusk.** The Door is Always Open
To those who Seek

VENTURE ADVENTURE

Above: **Going Green.** Some of today's cadets at the range -Marksman Pending?

Squadron Commanders

19??	Flt Lt A Cole RAFVR(T)
1954	Flt Lt B Storr RAFVR(T)
1956	Flt Lt A Ibbitson RAFVR(T)*
1962	Flt Lt J Taylor RAFVR(T)
1969	Flt Lt R Jones DSO DFC RAFVR(T)**
1977	Flt Lt S Close RAFVR(T)***
1981	Flt Lt D Crozier RAFVR(T)
1993	Flt Lt B Adgar RAFVR(T)

Squadron Camps

1941	Little Rissington	1978	Waddington
1943	Leeming Bar	1979	Machrihanish
1944	Thornaby	**1980**	Waddington
1951	Saxton Morley	1981	Leeming
1953	Hanley	1982	Machrihanish
1954	Leconfield	1983	Boulmer
1955	Cardington	1984	Brize Norton
1956	Rufforth	1985	Leeming
1958	Kinloss	1986	Leuchars
1963	Leuchars	1987	Linton on Ouse
1964	Kinloss	1988	Church Fenton
1965	Manston	**1990**	Linton on Ouse
1966	Shawbury	1992	Linton on Ouse
1967	Gaydon	1993	Lossiemouth
1968	Wyton	1994	Stafford
1969	Fairford (South Cerney)	1995	Northolt
1970	Wattisham	1996	Lossiemouth
1971	Machrihanish	1997	Linton on Ouse / Warcop
1972	Manby	**2002**	Leuchars
1973	Waddington	2003	Lossiemouth
1974	Finningly	2004	Valley
1975	Linton-on-Ouse	2006	Valley
1976	Kinloss	2007	Cottesmore
1977	Scampton		

As far as research has revealed - from 1980's squadrons ceased to go to camp as a complete unit

*Flt Lt Ibbitson flew a variety of RAF aircraft during World War II

**Flt Lt Jones flew Hampden Bombers during World War II.

***Flt Lt Close was an Ex-Hurricane Pilot.

Flt Lt Hall (2ic) flew with 617 Sqn - The Dambusters.

Above: **Cadet Forces Medal.**

Presented on completion of 12 years service.

The **Cadet Forces Medal** is awarded to recognise long and efficient service by Commissioned Officers and non commissioned adult instructors of the UK Cadet Forces. It is awarded for 12 years service. Additional clasps are issued for every 6 years additional service. Medal is stamped in cupro-nickel in the form of a circular Medal bearing on the obverse the Crowned Effigy of the Sovereign and on the reverse the inscription "The Cadet Forces Medal", and a representation of a torch.

Above: **The Falcon.** 1938 - 2014. Still Flying.

About the Author

Dave Walmsley BA(Hons) CertEd(FE) GIFireE RAFVR(T)

Dave Walmsley has served in the Air Training Corps for over 25 years. He joined as a Civilian Instructor in 1989 and his first squadron was 2214 (USWORTH). He is currently a Flight Lieutenant on squadron staff. Commissioned in 1998 he went on to become CO 1338 (SEAHAM) squadron and then officer at 111 (SUNDERLAND) squadron. In 2010 he returned to Usworth squadron to oversee staff/cadet development & special projects.

Returning is apt. He was actually a cadet on the squadron circa 1969 rising to the dizzy heights of Senior Cadet. Well remembered camps were RAF Fairford & RAF Wattisham. Lightnings, Phantoms and Concord (Meeting Brian Trubshaw test pilot) being highpoints and of course winning the squadron efficiency shield - a first for that time.

A Graduate of the IFE – (Institution of Fire Engineers) he holds a BA(Hons) in Education, CertEd(FE), NEBOSH and IOSH. He is a serving officer (Flight Lieutenant) in the RAFVR(T) -Royal Air Force Volunteer Reserve (Training) branch. A holder of the Fire Brigade Long Service & Good Conduct Medal, (20 years) 30 years Certificate, Cadet Forces Medal, Queen's Golden Jubilee Medal and Queen's Diamond Jubilee Medal.

He is a founder member of the Washington History Society and Northern Writers Group.

Also by the Author: Tyne And Wear Fire & Rescue An Illustrated History